DANGER IN THE AIR

AS TOLD TO BEN EAST

ILLUSTRATED & DESIGNED BY JACK DAHL

EDITED BY JEROLYN NENTL AND DR. HOWARD SCHROEDER

Professor in Reading and Language Arts, Dept. of Elementary Education, Mankato State University

Library of Congress Cataloging in Publication Data

East, Ben
    Danger in the air, as told to Ben East.
    (Survival)
    SUMMARY: As he prepares for another day of deep-sea fishing and div-
ing, Les Tassell is unable to shake the feeling that danger awaits him
somewhere in the isolated Florida Keys.
    1. Boats and boating--Florida--Accidents and injuries--Juvenile
literature. (1. Storms. 2. Survival) I. Dahl, John I. II. Nentl, Jerolyn Ann. III.
Schroeder, Howard. IV. Title. V. Series.
GV776.F6E2   614.8'64   79-53774
ISBN 0-89686-047-7 lib. bdg.
ISBN 0-89686-055-8 pbk.

International Standard Book Numbers: Library of Congress
    0-89686-047-7 Library Bound   Catalog Number:
    0-89686-055-8 Paperback   79-53774

ABOUT THE AUTHOR...

Ben East has been an *Outdoor Life* staff editor since 1946. Born in south-eastern Michigan in 1898, and a lifelong resident of that state, he sold his first story to *Outers Recreation* (later absorbed by *Outdoor Life*) in 1921. In 1926 he began a career as a professional writer, becoming outdoor editor of Booth Newspapers, a chain of dailies in eight major Michigan cities outside Detroit.

He left the newspaper job on January 1, 1946, to become Midwest field editor of Outdoor Life. In 1966 he was advanced to senior field editor, a post from which he retired at the end of 1970. Since then he has continued to write for the magazine as a contributing field editor.

Growing up as a farm boy, he began fishing and hunting as soon as he could handle a cane pole and a .22 rifle. He has devoted sixty years to outdoor sports, travel, adventure, wildlife photography, writing and lecturing. Ben has covered much of the back country of North America, from the eastern seaboard to the Aleutian Islands of Alaska, and from the Canadian arctic to the southern United States. He has written more than one thousand magazine articles and eight books. Today his by-line is one of the best known of any outdoor writer in the country. His outstanding achievement in wildlife photography was the making of the first color film ever taken of the Alaskan sea otter, in the summer of 1941.

In recent years much of his writing has dealt with major conservation problems confronting the nation. He has produced hard-hitting and effective articles on such environmentally destructive practices as strip mining, channelization, unethical use of aircraft to take trophy game, political interference in wildlife affairs, the indiscriminate use of pesticides and the damming of wild and scenic rivers and streams.

In 1973, he was signally honored when the Michigan Senate and House of Representatives adopted a concurrent resolution, the legislature's highest tribute, recognizing him for his distinguished contribution to the conservation of natural resources.

A FOREWORD TO DANGER IN THE AIR

At the time he lost his boat the Don-Jo, in the Florida keys, Les Tassell was a manufacturer of hardware at Grand Rapids, Michigan. His hobbies were outdoor activities of almost any kind. I had lived and worked in Grand Rapids as a newspaper writer for twenty years. Les and I became good friends, because of our interest in wild animals and our enjoyment of fishing, boating, and other outdoor pastimes.

After I moved from Grand Rapids, I visited Les at his home. He told of an accident that had happened a few years before, in which his boat was wrecked. Both he and his wife Ruth, had a narrow escape from drowning. The story sounded exciting, but Les and I were talking about a trip he had made to Africa and another he was planning to India. We did not find time to talk about the boat mishap. When I left, I asked him to let me know more about it in a letter.

When the letter came it was seventeen pages long. The story was as interesting as I had expected. I visited Les again, took notes while he talked, and wrote the story as he told it to me.

Les had another exciting hobby. He started a game park on thirty-five acres of fenced land by his home near Grand Rapids. It was stocked with buffalo, deer, and elk. The deer were the hardest to get. They were running at large on a neighboring game farm, and the owner told Les, "there they are, you catch'em."

One of the most interesting things this sportsman ever did was tame a pair of Zebras he got from Africa. He broke them to harness, and trained them to pull a buggy as horses do.

BEN EAST

Les Tassell awoke from a deep sleep with a chilling sense that something was wrong. He lay quietly in his berth, listening. The ship's clock chimed midnight. There was no other sound to disturb the stillness of the Florida night. It was so calm he could not even hear the usual lapping of the water against the Don-Jo's planking. There was no hint of trouble of any kind, but Les felt uneasy.

He slipped out of his berth and walked up on deck. All was shipshape, just as he and his wife and first mate had left it when they went below two hours earlier. It was a fine night. The velvet sky was sprinkled with stars that seemed close enough to touch. The sea was smooth as glass, and the Don-Jo lay still on the black water. The sea was so calm that the boat did not even tug at its anchors. Black against the sky a thousand feet to the south was Content Key. In the night it was only a low outline broken by mangrove trees and a few scrub palms. There was not even a surf to break on the ragged coral beach.

There could not have been a more peaceful scene. Since all was snug and safe, Les went below and turned in once again. Yet he could not shake the haunting feeling that something was wrong. He tried to sleep, but his mind wandered. He could only doze.

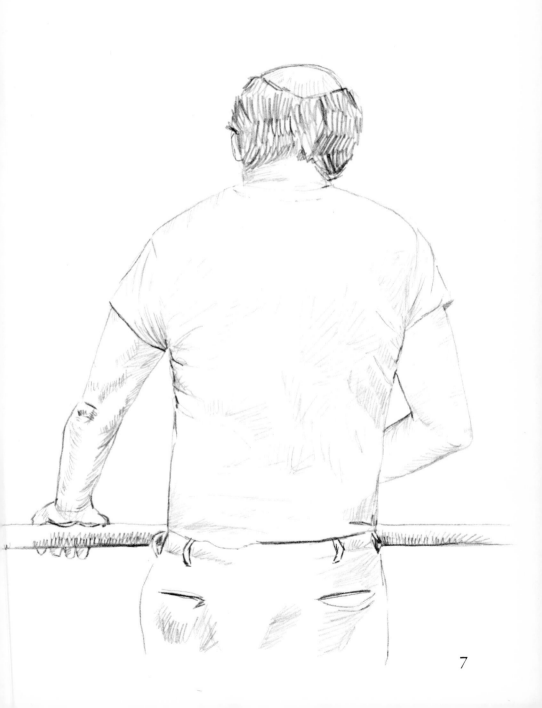

7

The cruise to this beautiful stretch of water had begun two years earlier in Michigan. It took shape at the Tassell's home in Grand Rapids. Les and his wife, Ruth, owned a thirty-three-foot cruiser they moored at Holland, on Lake Michigan. They had enjoyed many good times on the boat with their friends and wished they could use it more often. They also wanted to escape the long cold winters of the north. Les liked to fish and wanted to enjoy his sport more. So they planned to move the Don-Jo's home port to Florida. Fort Lauderdale looked like a good spot.

9

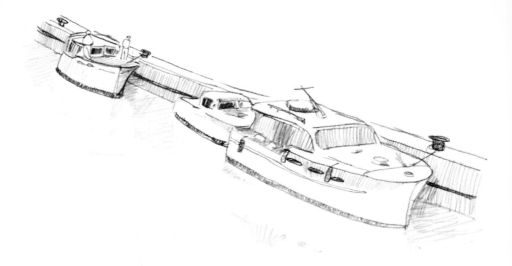

They set out across Lake Michigan, sailed the Illinois ship canal to the Mississippi River, and took the big river as far as Cairo. From there the couple sailed up the Ohio River, and weaved their way through a series of lakes to Guntersville. There the trip by water ended for awhile. The Don-Jo had to be moved by truck where Les and Ruth met her, and cruised down Florida's inland waterway.

Les smiled while resting, as he thought of those first days in port. He and Ruth were busy outfitting the Don-Jo for deep-sea fishing. They had hired Ed Boshead as first mate to free Les from the full time job of running the boat. Les wanted to be able to fish as much as he could. It had been a good time, fun and full of laughter. He did not understand this feeling of doom that was nagging at him as he tried to sleep. He still just dozed, his mind wandering over the events of those first days in Florida.

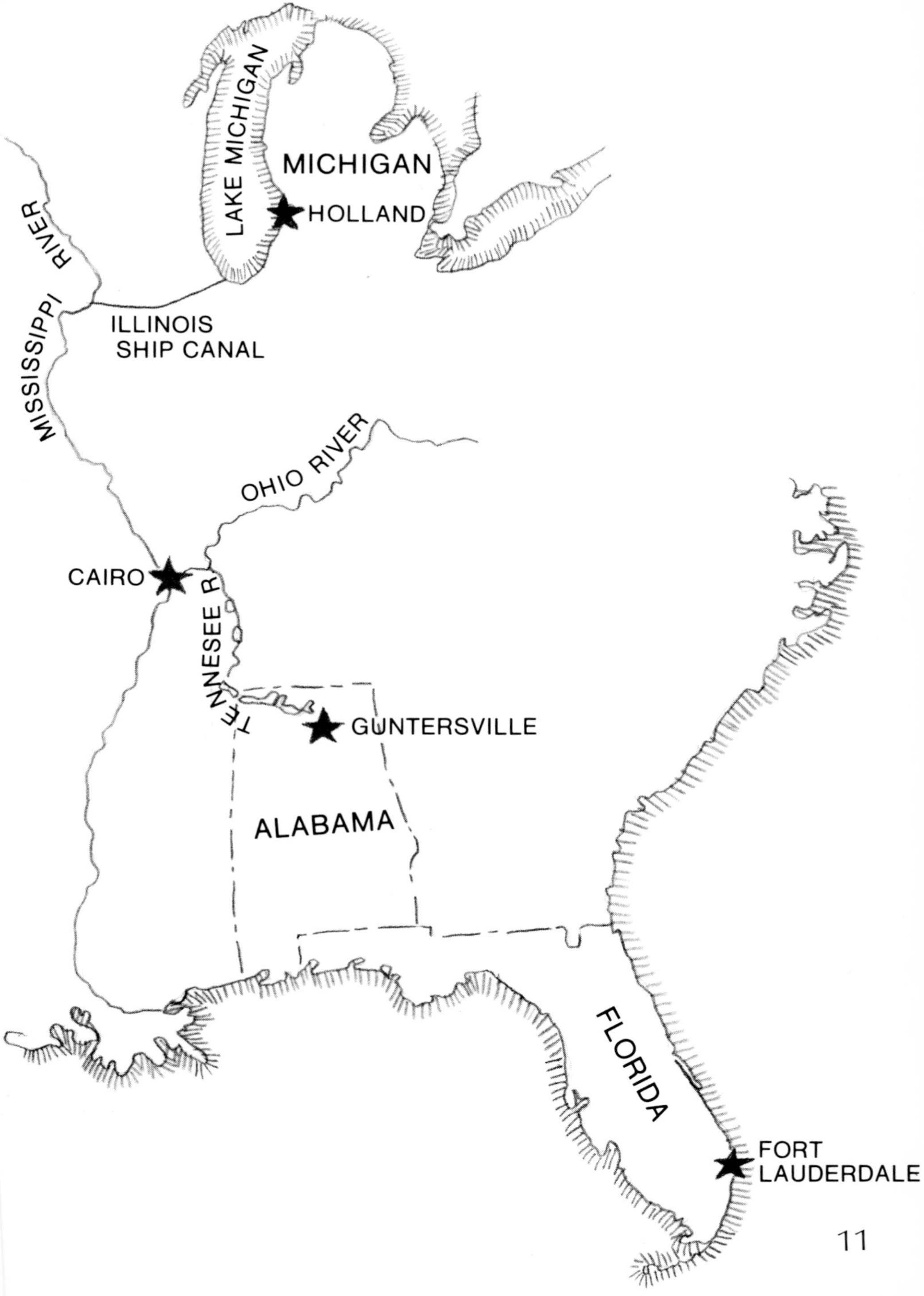

LAKE MICHIGAN

MICHIGAN

★ HOLLAND

MISSISSIPPI RIVER

ILLINOIS
SHIP CANAL

OHIO RIVER

CAIRO ★

TENNESEE R.

★ GUNTERSVILLE

ALABAMA

FLORIDA

★ FORT
LAUDERDALE

11

The three had traveled south into the Keys. "Keys" is the term the Florida natives use for the small islands that dot the sea off the southern tip of their state. They took the Don-Jo west, to Marathon. Les had been told that there was good deep-sea fishing near there. The tales were true, too. For two weeks he had sampled just about every kind of fish he could imagine. There were kings, dolphins, and jack crevalle. Between trips out to the deep water, it

13

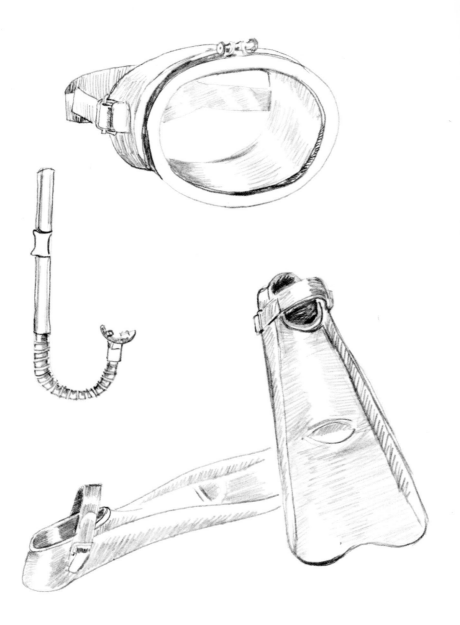

14

was always fun to loaf on deck with Ruth. Ed was telling tales of a sport new to them. It was skin diving. The more Ed told about the world under the sea, the more Les wanted to see it for himself.

So they made a trip into port. Les bought fins, a snorkel mask and a spear, then practiced in a pool near the beach. Slowly he got the feel of being under water.

The pleasant dreams did not dispel Les' feeling that something was wrong. In the calm night he continued to toss and turn in his berth. The uneasy feeling would not go away. He still could not sleep, but he dozed once again.

This morning they had backed the Don-Jo from the dock and headed west and north. It had been fine, clear weather. It was no wonder the night had turned out to be so beautiful. They were headed for a small dot of coral and mangrove known as Content Key. Those in port, who knew the sea well, had told them there was no better place in all the Keys.

The run was as nice as any Les could recall. There had not been a cloud in the sky. The waters of Florida Bay from the mainland to the Keys were still. Not a breeze ruffled the surface. Porpoises played in the clear blue water and clumsy brown pelicans soared high in the sky. Once in a while one of the big birds would draw in its wings and dive straight into the sea. An instant later it would reappear and gulp down a fish. The Don-Jo's engines purred like

contented cats. Les relaxed at the wheel while Ed busied himself with some minor chores. Ruth soaked up the sun on the afterdeck. It had been one of those perfect days in the middle of the Florida winter. It felt extra warm when Les thought of the cold winter up north.

He had run the Don-Jo far out into the bay. Then he made a wide turn so he could approach Content Key from the north. His charts showed deep channels banked by coral reefs all the way to the Key. He looked carefully at the water. The surface colors proved the charts right. It had been tempting fishing water, but Les kept the boat going. He was in a hurry to get to Content Key and was anxious to try his luck at skin diving.

Content Key lay just a few feet above the sea at high tide. It was a low blob of gray coral when the three first caught a glimpse of it. On the south side it sloped down into a mangrove swamp. Les slowed the Don-Jo's engines to look things over. There was a series of coral reefs leading up to the beach. Only eight to ten feet of water covered them, but there were deep channels in between. Les was able to get the boat within three hundred yards of the beach. They dropped the bow anchor at that point and backed off about fifty yards to drop stern anchor. There was a light offshore breeze, but Les knew the two anchors would keep the boat from rocking back and forth. The rest of the day had been spent exploring the Key and water around it.

Les was still restless as he lay in his berth. The pleasant dreams did not ward off the chilling sense that something was wrong. What could it be in this peaceful place? Why couldn't he sleep? His mind wandered back to his dreams, and he dozed once more.

Les and Ed liked what they had glimpsed of the ocean floor as they approached the Key. There were lots of deep holes and dark caves under the coral ledges. They were anxious to get a closer look, so the two put on swim trunks and took out the eight foot dinghy. It was only a short while before Ed had given Les the nod. They had come to just the right spot for what they had in mind. The shallow waters were filled with fish. There were kinds they couldn't even name. In the shoals offshore from the swamp they rowed over manta rays as wide as the dinghy was long. The dark, ugly creatures looked like bats sprawled flat on the ocean floor. Two or three times they had seen the tall dorsal fins of cruising sharks cut the water around them. There would be plenty of excitement here! But first, Les and Ed made an agreement. They would leave the big fish alone until Les had some ocean diving practice. Ed assured Les that even a beginner would see lots of action in a spot like this. The coral reefs and the many kinds of fish made it a good site. By the time they were through rowing around the Key, it was too late in the day to dive. So they went back to the Don-Jo to eat dinner and plan the next day.

Les turned over in his berth again. The evening had been as fine as the day. He did not know why he still felt something was wrong. But once more he only dozed, thinking of last evening.

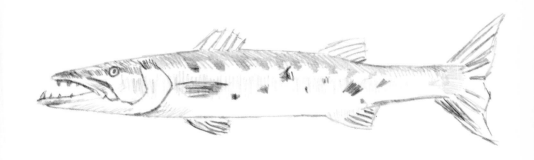

GREAT BARRACUDA

ATLANTIC MANTA

While the three ate dinner, the light breeze died and the sea turned to glass. The stars gave almost as much light as a young moon. And when darkness fell, the night residents of the coral reefs put on quite a show. Tiny shrimp swam to the surface by the thousands to mate, looking like glowworms in the sea. They swam up in pairs, spawned, then drifted back down from where they had come. All the while they lit the sea with their strange light. From out of nowhere a school of minnows looking to feed would slash through the shrimp. Alarmed, the shrimp would scatter. On the heels of the minnows would come a pack of yellowtails. Once they passed, the sea would grow still until the cycle began again.

The three stayed awake for hours, watching and talking. At ten o'clock, Les took a last look at the two anchor lines and made a mental note of the location and outline of the Key. Then they turned in for a good night's sleep.

Les had tossed and turned in his berth for more than an hour since waking up at midnight. He wanted very much to go to sleep. He was tired, and knew there was a big day of skin diving ahead. He lay back on his berth, relaxed, and fell asleep.

He did not sleep for long.

Suddenly wind was pounding rain against the Don-Jo's windows! The boat was rolling and pitching at her anchor lines like a bucking horse! Les raced for the deck. When he stepped out of the cabin the wind tore at him. The hissing rain almost blinded him. Les knew that sudden squalls are common in the Keys and that they pass quickly. He was sure the Don-Jo could withstand an ordinary storm with no danger, so he tried to remain calm. He rubbed the water from his eyes and looked toward Content Key. What he saw through the storm made his hair stand on end! The tiny island was much closer than it had been at ten o'clock. The Don-Jo was being driven onshore by the wind! She was dragging her anchors!

Les ducked his head back into the cabin.

"Roll out," he yelled to Ruth and Ed. "We're going aground!"

Ruth and Ed were on deck in seconds. They all knew there was only one thing to do — head for the open sea. Les kicked the engines alive. Ed started to bring in the stern anchor line. At his cry of "Anchor up!" Les threw in the clutch. The engines roared full speed ahead. The boat charged into the seas, straining at the impact.

Then a shudder ran the length of the Don-Jo. The starboard engine sputtered and quit. Les knew

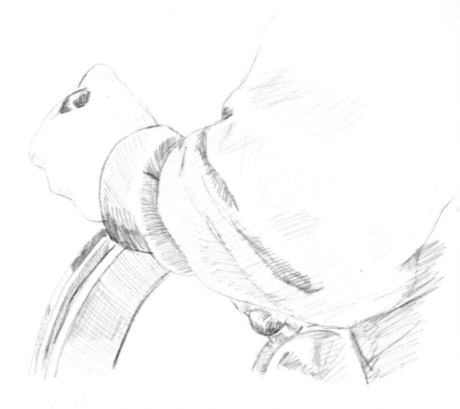

what was wrong before Ed shouted the word. In the
dark, a loop of anchor line had slid into the sea. It
had been sucked into the starboard engine and had
fouled it. The Don-Jo was on one engine now, and
Les knew before he tried that one engine was not
enough. He kept her on full throttle, but the Don-Jo
was still being blown toward the bow anchor. Ed
scrambled to get it up while Les fought the wheel.
He tried to turn the boat around and head her
offshore. It was no use. With a jolting crash, she
struck the reef. Les, Ruth, and Ed lost their footing
and fell to the deck. A second later the next wave

ADULT

ATLANTIC-PACIFIC

NO 160

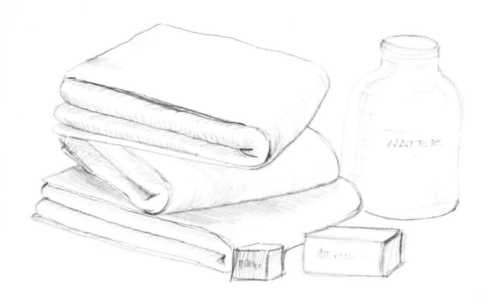

lifted the Don-Jo and smashed her down again. They could hear her ribs and planking splinter as the storm pounded her on the coral. No boat could take such a beating for long.

"It's time to get ashore," Les shouted.

He knew Ruth and Ed were thinking the same thing. Could they make it to the beach in such seas? They kept the thought to themselves, and quickly put on their life jackets. No one said a word. Ed and Les loosened the dinghy and slid it down from its cradle on top of the cabin. They grabbed blankets, food, and a few clothes and strapped them in the little boat. Ruth found their large jug of fresh drinking water and put it with the rest of the gear. By the time they had the dinghy ready the deck was awash. The wind was blowing black sheets of rain over the top of the cabin. The Don-Jo was low in the water now. Each wave lifted her, tilting her first to one crazy angle and then another. The boat was slowly breaking apart. They knew they could not row to the Key. The little eight foot dinghy would not stay afloat a minute in such a surf with three aboard. If they were to reach the beach at all, they would have to get into the water with the dinghy.

They shoved the little boat off the tilting deck and slid into the water beside it. The true fury of the sea startled them. They clung to the dinghy — floating, swimming and crawling. They knew there was one thing in their favor. The same wind that had driven the Don-Jo aground would also carry them to shore. If they could just keep their grip on the dinghy and not get cut to shreds by the sharp coral, the storm would put them on the beach.

A great wave lifted them, almost tearing the boat from their hands. Then it threw them down and left them to float in the raging water until the next one caught them. Again and again the sea pushed and pulled them. Les glanced back at the Don-Jo. It was far behind them. They walked the last fifty yards, with the crashing waves tugging at their legs. They dragged the dinghy with them, carrying it when they could. They knew they must beach it un-

31

damaged if it were to help them get off the Key
when the storm calmed. They stumbled and slipped
and fell. The coral cut their feet. But at last there
was no surf around their ankles. They were bruised
and battered. They were fighting for breath, feeling
half drowned. But they were ashore!

33

They pulled the dinghy under a clump of mangroves; however, the scraggly trees gave little shelter from the storm. The three were chilled to the bone and had to wrap themselves in blankets to keep warm. There was no way to start a fire. Turning the dinghy on its side, they huddled behind it to get out of the howling wind. The time passed slowly. Crabs in the mangroves made a snapping noise that made the peaceful Key seem very fierce at night. Above the noise of the storm they could also hear the sea pounding the life out of their boat. They could do nothing but listen helplessly.

At last daylight began to glow in the eastern sky. The storm began to ease, but the rain and heavy surf continued. When the sea calmed, Les and Ed rowed out to have a closer look at what was left of the Don-Jo. The upper hull and cabin did not look too bad, but Les knew better than to hope for much. When they got on board they found her a total loss, just as he had expected. Her bottom was torn out and the engines were smashed. The screws and shafts were twisted into scrap metal and everthing left loose inside her had been carried away by the raging sea. She was a gutted boat! Since there was nothing that could be done with her, they rowed sadly back to the island and shared a cold snack with Ruth while thinking how to get off Content Key.

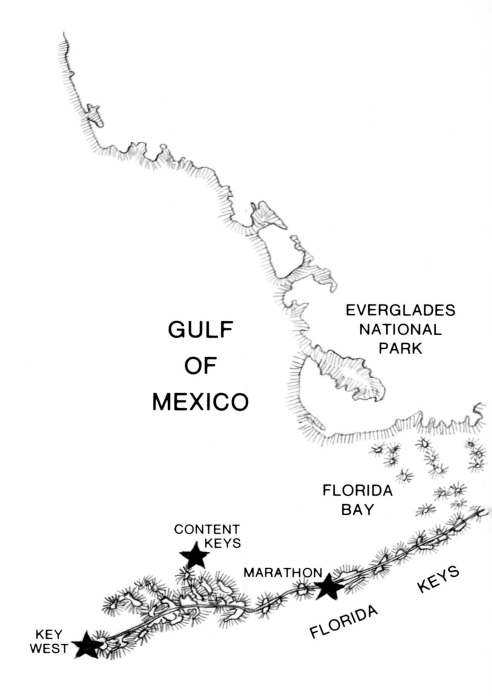

GULF
OF
MEXICO

EVERGLADES
NATIONAL
PARK

FLORIDA
BAY

CONTENT
KEYS

MARATHON

KEYS

KEY
WEST

FLORIDA

The dinghy could not hold all of them, even in calm seas. Someone would have to go for help. It would be a long row, since no one lived in the Keys. The nearest chance to meet someone would be along U.S. Highway 1, the bridge-and-causeway road that leads from the mainland to Key West. That was twenty miles down the Spanish Channel. It was open sea. The water would be far from smooth, but the reefs would break the worst of it. The wind would be with the little boat all the way.

Ed said he would go.

"I'll be back with a rescue boat of some kind before dark," he promised.

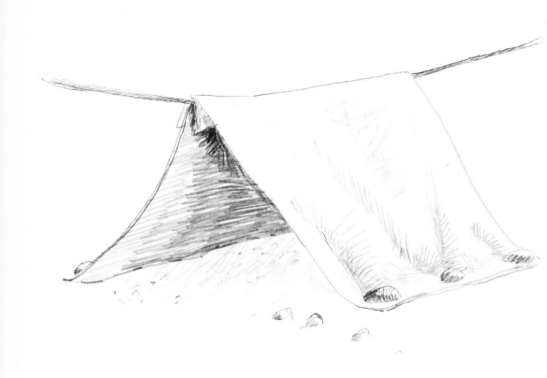

Les and Ruth watched him shove off. They watched until the boat looked no bigger than a two-legged beetle crawling across the gray sea. Then they busied themselves with gathering what little wood could be found on the island. They also put up two blankets to form a crude tent. They knew Ed might not be able to keep his promise.

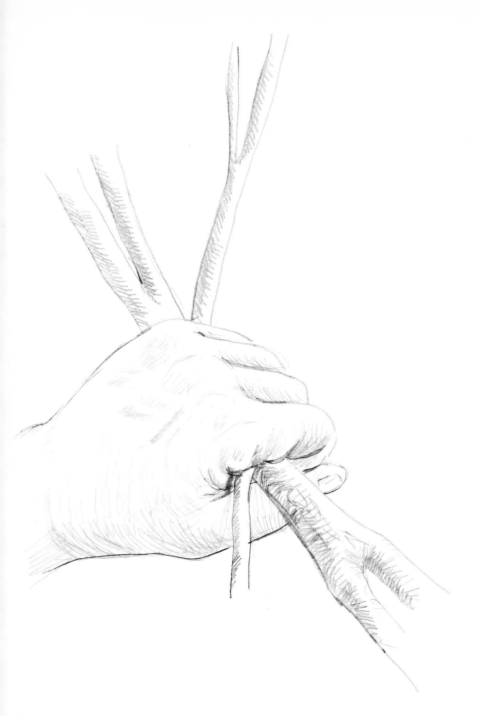

41

It took only a short while to finish their simple chores. Then they explored the Key which did not take long since it was such a small island. There was no sign that anyone had spent time on the Key. Les and Ruth could not think of one reason why anyone would.

Time passed slowly. When the afternoon was almost gone and there was no sign of Ed, the two began to get ready for a second night on the island. They had food, water and wood for a fire. It was Ed they worried about. Could he make it across twenty miles of open sea in a rowboat without mishap?

44

They were piling up a small heap of dry wood
for a fire when they heard a welcome sound. In the
distance was the hum of a big outboard motor! It
came from the other side of the Key. They ran for
the beach just in time to see a skiff planing in,
throwing a high wedge of spray as it roared across
the water.

Ed had been lucky. He had been found by Speck Smith, who lived in a cottage by the highway. Ed was exhausted and hungry when Speck found him. But his only concern had been getting Ruth and Les off the Key before nightfall. He was with Speck in the skiff to make sure they were both all right. In less than an hour they were all back at the road. Their trying experience was finished as quickly as it had started.

What was it Les Tassell felt in his sleep that night off Content Key? What awoke him so abruptly? Why could he not go back to sleep? Les thinks it was a premonition. Some people don't believe in them, but Les does. He sometimes calls it just a hunch. At times he credits it to his guardian angel. But more than once in his life, Les says he has felt a strong sense of doom. It is like an advance warning that something is going to happen.

Les felt it that calm, winter night in Florida Bay. If he had paid attention, they all might have missed a terrible experience.

They might also have saved a good boat.

Stay on the edge of your seat.

Read:

FROZEN TERROR

DANGER IN THE AIR

MISTAKEN JOURNEY

TRAPPED IN DEVIL'S HOLE

DESPERATE SEARCH

FORTY DAYS LOST

FOUND ALIVE

GRIZZLY!

SURVIVAL

TRUE STORIES